D0745580

BIGGEST NAMES IN SPORTS
LUKA DONCIC
BASKETBALL STAR

by Alex Monnig

FOCUS
READERS.
NAVIGATOR

WWW.FOCUSREADERS.COM

Focus Readers is distributed by North Star Editions:
sales@northstareditions.com | 888-417-0195

Produced for Focus Readers by Red Line Editorial.

Photographs ©: Eric Christian Smith/AP Images, cover, 1; Jim Mone/AP Images, 4–5, 7; David Berding/Getty Images Sport/Getty Images, 9; Matej Kastelic/Shutterstock Images, 10–11; Ints Kalnins/Reuters/Newscom, 12; Edwin yordany/Shutterstock Images, 15; LevanteMedia/Shutterstock Images, 16–17; Luca Sgamellotti/Euroleague Basketball/Getty Images, 19; Rokas Tenys/Shutterstock Images, 21; Kevin Hagen/AP Images, 22–23; Matt York/AP Images, 25; John Hefti/AP Images, 27; Red Line Editorial, 29

Library of Congress Cataloging-in-Publication Data
Library of Congress Cataloging-in-Publication Data is available on the Library of Congress website.

ISBN
978-1-64493-052-6 (hardcover)
978-1-64493-131-8 (paperback)
978-1-64493-289-6 (ebook pdf)
978-1-64493-210-0 (hosted ebook)

Printed in the United States of America
Mankato, MN
012020

ABOUT THE AUTHOR

Alex Monnig is a freelance journalist from St. Louis, Missouri, who now lives in Sydney, Australia. He graduated with a master's degree from the University of Missouri in 2010. During his career, he has spent time covering sporting events around the world and has written more than 20 children's books.

TABLE OF CONTENTS

CHAPTER 1

Taking the Lead 5

CHAPTER 2

Growing Up in the Gym 11

CHAPTER 3

Raising His Game 17

CHAPTER 4

Instant Impact 23

At-a-Glance Map • 28

Focus on Luka Doncic • 30

Glossary • 31

To Learn More • 32

Index • 32

TAKING THE LEAD

Luka Doncic was only 19 years old. But he was already leading the Dallas Mavericks. Doncic and the Mavs trailed the Minnesota Timberwolves 111–110 in a 2019 regular-season game. The clock showed 1:41 to go in the fourth quarter. The game was in Minnesota, so everyone was cheering for the Wolves.

Doncic dribbles past a Timberwolves defender in January 2019.

Doncic dribbled near mid-court and sized up the defense. Then he attacked. As Doncic **drove** toward the basket, Minnesota center Karl-Anthony Towns matched him step for step. But Doncic jumped off his left foot, floating away from Towns. Doncic hung in the air and waited until the last possible moment to release his shot. It fell in for a basket.

Dallas led 112–111 with 1:28 on the clock. But the Wolves scored another basket to retake the lead. The Minnesota crowd roared.

With about a minute left, Doncic again started near mid-court. And again he attacked. Doncic jumped toward the

Doncic throws down a monster slam dunk against the Timberwolves.

hoop, slicing through two defenders. He threw down a two-handed dunk to give the Mavericks a one-point lead. The crowd went quiet. But then the Wolves answered with a basket of their own.

Minnesota was clinging to a 115–114 lead with only 26 seconds left.

Doncic dribbled up the court. It looked like he was going to drive again. Towns, the closest defender, took a step back to guard the drive. But Doncic pulled up behind the three-point line and let it fly.

MORE LATE HEROICS

Minnesota was not the only team Luka Doncic dominated during the 2018–19 season. Against the Houston Rockets, he went on an amazing 11–0 run late in the game. His performance helped Dallas come back from an eight-point deficit. Doncic also hit a game-tying three-pointer against the Portland Trail Blazers that season.

Doncic celebrates after making a huge three-pointer against the Timberwolves.

The net barely moved as the shot splashed in. Dallas led 117–115 with 23 seconds left. Doncic slapped his legs in triumph. The Mavericks held on to win the game. And it wouldn't have been possible without their star **rookie**.

CHAPTER 2

GROWING UP IN THE GYM

Luka Doncic was born in Ljubljana, Slovenia, on February 28, 1999. His journey to the National Basketball Association (NBA) started early. Sports were in Luka's blood. His mother was a hurdler and dancer. His father played basketball professionally in Europe. And his godfather played in the NBA.

Ljubljana, the capital of Slovenia, is home to approximately 280,000 people.

Luka's father, Sasa (left), competes in a game with Union Olimpija in 2007.

Luka had a basketball in his hands from the time he was seven months old. His mother put a toy hoop in his room when he was just a year old. Even at that age, he was making shots.

Luka wiped the floors and was the **ball boy** at many of his father's basketball games. At halftime, he often shot as much as he could before the players came back out. His shooting **technique** was advanced for his age. He had his father's feel for the game.

Luka moved smoothly around the court. He was far better than the other kids his age. So he played with older kids who were bigger and faster. That forced Luka to beat them with his brain rather than his speed.

In 2007, at age eight, Luka joined the Union Olimpija basketball school. He spent the next four years playing older opponents. Even so, Luka was the star. He threw behind-the-back passes and scored in bunches.

The youngster's talent was becoming legendary. But Luka's career really took off when he became a teenager. That's when he received an offer to play for Spanish club Real Madrid.

The decision was tough. Madrid was hundreds of miles from his family and

RAPID RISE

It did not take long for Luka to impress the coaches at Union Olimpija. Just 16 minutes into his first practice, the coaches moved him to an older group. And after just one practice there, they bumped him up to the Union Olimpija selection team. There he played against kids who were three to four years older.

Madrid is the capital of Spain. It is approximately 1,250 miles (2,000 km) from Ljubljana.

friends in Slovenia. And he did not speak Spanish. Luka thought about it for weeks. But the chance to improve his skills was too good to pass up. Luka packed up and moved to Spain. It was there he became a superstar.

RAISING HIS GAME

At age 13, Luka Doncic moved to Spain to follow his basketball dreams. Now it was time to make those dreams a reality. He had all the skills. However, living in a foreign country was difficult at first. For starters, he could not speak Spanish. But Luka worked hard to learn the language.

Luka takes the ball down the court during a 2016 game with Real Madrid.

Luka shined in the 2013 Minicopa, a tournament for younger players. He was named most valuable player (MVP). As usual, he was outplaying older boys. But now he was doing it in Spain. That country has one of the top basketball leagues in the world. Within two years, it was clear that Luka was ready for the next level.

Luka made his **debut** for the Real Madrid senior team in April 2015. At just 16 years old, he was the youngest Real Madrid player ever. He played in only three league games that season. But there was no doubt that he would be back the next season.

Luka accepts the trophy after winning a tournament with Real Madrid.

In 2015–16, Luka played in 43 games for Real Madrid. Some of those games were part of Liga ACB, the top league in Spain. Other games were part of the EuroLeague. This league features the best club teams from across Europe.

Luka really broke out during the 2016–17 season. He won the EuroLeague Rising Star Award. He also took home the Liga ACB Best Young Player Award.

Doncic reached yet another level in the 2017–18 season. He averaged 14.5 points, 5.2 rebounds, and 4.6 assists per game.

LEARNING FROM THE BEST

Before Doncic moved to North America, he learned about the NBA from his teammates. At Real Madrid, he played with former NBA players Rudy Fernandez and Andres Nocioni. And on the Slovenian national team, he played alongside NBA All-Star Goran Dragic. When Doncic was growing up, he had been a huge fan of Dragic.

Doncic attempts a layup during a 2017 EuroLeague game.

Real Madrid won the EuroLeague that season. And Doncic became the youngest player to win the EuroLeague MVP.

The Slovenian had shown his skills in Europe. Now he was ready to test himself against the best players in the world. It was time to enter the NBA **Draft**.

CHAPTER 4

INSTANT IMPACT

Just two days after winning the EuroLeague title, Luka Doncic flew to New York City for the 2018 NBA Draft. He didn't have to wait long to hear his name called. The Atlanta Hawks chose Doncic third overall. A few minutes later, the Hawks traded him to the Dallas Mavericks. Doncic was heading to Texas.

Doncic shakes hands with the NBA commissioner after being drafted by the Hawks.

When Doncic arrived in Dallas, he learned a lot from Mavs teammate Dirk Nowitzki. Many basketball fans believe that Nowitzki was the best foreign NBA player of all time. Nowitzki came from Germany. He knew what it was like to enter the NBA at a young age with high expectations. Doncic was excited to play with an all-time great.

Doncic's first NBA game was one to forget. He scored just 10 points in a loss to the Phoenix Suns. But there weren't many nights like that during his rookie season. Doncic scored an impressive 26 points in his second game. He was off and running.

A 19-year-old Doncic competes in his first NBA game in October 2018.

Doncic quickly became the team's go-to player. Mavs fans loved his ability to come through in the **clutch**. Basketball experts compared him to NBA greats such as James Harden, Kyrie Irving, and Kevin Durant.

The all-around game that Doncic mastered in Spain was a perfect fit for the NBA. He could score. He could rebound. He could set up his teammates. Doncic finished the season averaging 21.2 points, 7.8 rebounds, and 6.0 assists. With numbers like that, it was no surprise

NOT QUITE AN ALL-STAR

Doncic was one of the best players in the first half of the 2018–19 NBA season. He earned the third-most All-Star votes from fans. But fans' votes count for only half of the total. The other half comes from sportswriters, coaches, and players. They did not give Doncic the votes he needed to make the team. His All-Star dreams would have to wait.

Doncic tries to make a play during a 2019 game against the Golden State Warriors.

that he was named NBA Rookie of the Year. Doncic had made it to the NBA. And he appeared to have a very bright future ahead of him.

LUKA DONCIC

- Height: 6 feet 7 inches (201 cm)
- Weight: 218 pounds (99 kg)
- Birth date: February 28, 1999
- Birthplace: Ljubljana, Slovenia
- Minor league teams: Union Olimpija (2007–12)
- Pro teams: Real Madrid (2015–18); Dallas Mavericks (2018–)
- Major awards: EuroLeague Rising Star (2017, 2018); Liga ACB Best Young Player (2017, 2018); Liga ACB champion (2015, 2016, 2018); EuroBasket champion (2017); EuroLeague champion (2018); EuroLeague MVP (2018); NBA Rookie of the Year (2019)

FOCUS ON
LUKA DONCIC

Write your answers on a separate piece of paper.

1. Write a paragraph explaining the main ideas of Chapter 3.

2. Do you think Doncic would have been good at basketball if he had different parents? Why or why not?

3. What team did Luka Doncic join at age eight?

> **A.** Real Madrid
> **B.** Union Olimpija
> **C.** Dallas Mavericks

4. Why did Doncic move from Slovenia to Spain when he was young?

> **A.** He was sick of living in Slovenia.
> **B.** Spain had a better basketball league.
> **C.** Most of his friends were in Spain.

Answer key on page 32.

GLOSSARY

ball boy

A person who chases loose balls and gives new balls to players and officials.

clutch

A difficult situation when the outcome of the game is in question.

debut

First appearance.

draft

A system that allows teams to acquire new players coming into a league.

drove

Dribbled hard toward a certain area on the court.

rookie

A professional athlete in his or her first year.

technique

The way a person performs certain movements, usually to do a specific job.

TO LEARN MORE

BOOKS

Bryant, Howard. *Legends: The Best Players, Games, and Teams in Basketball*. New York: Philomel Books, 2017.

Graves, Will. *NBA's Top 10 Rookies*. Minneapolis: Abdo Publishing, 2018.

Whiting, Jim. *Dallas Mavericks*. Mankato, MN: Creative Education, 2018.

NOTE TO EDUCATORS

Visit **www.focusreaders.com** to find lesson plans, activities, links, and other resources related to this title.

INDEX

Atlanta Hawks, 23

Dragic, Goran, 20

EuroLeague, 19–21, 23

Houston Rockets, 8

Liga ACB, 19–20
Ljubljana, Slovenia, 11

Minicopa, 18
Minnesota
  Timberwolves, 5–8

National Basketball
  Association (NBA),
  11, 20, 24–27
NBA Draft, 21, 23
Nowitzki, Dirk, 24

Phoenix Suns, 24

Portland Trail Blazers,
  8

Real Madrid, 14, 18–21

Towns, Karl-Anthony,
  6, 8

Union Olimpija, 13–14